ON LINE TO SUCCESS

GW00634928

THE AUTHOR

Denis McMahon was born in Listowel, Co. Kerry, in 1941, and graduated from UCD in 1961 with a first-class honours degree in economics and politics. His entire working career has been spent in the computer industry, in Ireland and in Britain. In 1979 he set up his own company, Online Computing Ltd, and developed it into a highly successful business; some ten years later he sold Online and retired from the computer industry.

DENIS McMAHON

ON LINE TO

SUCCESS

BUSINESS
POOLBEG

A Paperback Original
First published 1993 by
Poolbeg Press Ltd
Knocksedan House,
Swords, Co Dublin, Ireland

© Denis A. McMahon 1993

The moral right of the author has been asserted.

A catalogue record for this book is available from the British Library.

ISBN 1 85371 253 1

All rights reserved. No part of this publication may be reproduced or transmitted in any form or by
any means, electronic or mechanical, including photography, recording, or any information storage
or retrieval system, without permission in writing from the publisher. The book is sold subject to the
condition that it shall not, by way of trade or otherwise, be lent, resold or otherwise circulated
without the publisher's prior consent in any form of binding or cover other than that in which it is
published and without a similar condition including this condition being imposed on the
subsequent purchaser.

Cover design by Pomphrey Associates
Set by Mac Book Limited in Stone 9.5
Printed by The Guernsey Press Company Ltd,
Vale, Guernsey, Channel Islands

To Margaret,
for her contribution to this story and whose love,
encouragement and constant support helped to make it a
reality.

Contents

Preface

I started my own business in July 1979. From the moment I left college in the early 1960s I spent my entire working career in the computer industry. In those days it was an exciting, fast-growing and very rewarding business to work in. For anyone who had the expertise and could deliver the goods, the rewards were above average: high salaries, generous expense accounts, a company car, pensionable employment, and of course job security. In many respects it was an environment that was so cosy that it produced an aversion to risk-taking. So why take the plunge?

For my own part, I had always at the back of my mind nurtured an ambition to be my own boss, to set up and run my own company and to put into practice my own business standards. What I needed was a trigger that would force my hand and propel me into action. That came in the form of a growing frustration at the way the company I then worked for was conducting its business. Orders in the buoyant computer market were relatively easy to secure; but the quality and reliability of the product and the levels of customer service being provided left a lot to be desired. This was due more to a problem of attitude rather than a lack of the necessary skills and expertise. There was a low focus on the needs and importance of the customer and his or her entitlement to receive a solution that worked, one that was delivered on time and was backed up by an acceptable and reliable standard of after-sales service.

I might add that this particular deficiency was one

that was prevalent in many indigenous industries at that time, and still exists to this day. It is quite staggering to see the extent to which many businesses fail to acknowledge the basic principle that the customer is the one who butters the bread, and who calls the shots.

Having endured the increasing frustration of trying to cope with this environment, I began to realise that for me it also represented a business opportunity: to do it myself, and do it right. So in 1979 I left the secure, pensionable and well-paid job, and in July of that year Online Computing was born.

It was a decision I was never to regret. What followed were ten glorious years of endeavour and achievement—years of careful planning and thorough preparation, of aggressive marketing and selling, of tight financial controls, of controlled growth, of a strong work ethic, of close attention to customer needs and service, and of constant preoccupation with the bottom line. In 1989 I sold the business and became a relatively wealthy man.

To anyone with a good business idea and a desire to set up their own business I would say—do it. Believe me, nothing concentrates the mind more than putting your own money, your own reputation, your own pride and self-esteem on the line. You will discover a depth of personal resource you never even imagined you possessed. You will experience the exhilarations of success and the agonies of setbacks and failures in a much more personal way than before. The satisfaction and fulfilment to be derived from taking a raw business concept, putting it into operation and developing it into a successful venture cannot be matched in any other business context.

But a word of caution. The world the entrepreneur operates in is not an easy one. Running a business was never a simple or straightforward task; in today's complex and highly competitive business world it is an even more daunting challenge. To be successful there are certain essential prerequisites that every aspiring entrepreneur starting out should take on board: do it and give it everything you've got, but, most importantly, go about it in a well-organised, carefully planned and thoroughly professional way. Through careful planning and thorough preparation, through following certain basic procedures and business principles, you will minimise the risks and optimise your chances of success. Preparation, planning and professionalism are key ingredients to success. If you are going to do it, then do it properly.

This book sets out certain guidelines in a simple and straightforward way that are aimed at just that: doing it properly. It is based on my own personal experiences as an entrepreneur over a ten-year period and incorporates the many sound disciplines, principles and procedures that played a key role in our business success. It is not the theory of business management but rather the reality. Believe me, it works.

Part 1

Preparing for Take-off

1

The Idea

Every journey into business must begin with a business idea. This need not be original, innovative, spectacular, or even different. Very few people are lucky enough to be born innovators, capable of pioneering a brand-new concept and translating it into a successful business venture. Most of us must look around us for ideas, and we are most likely to find them in our own work environment. Whether we are involved in production or in sales, in distribution or in marketing, in finance or in management, in customer support or in research, new ideas and opportunities will, from time to time, suggest themselves to us. If one or more of these ideas persists and begins to acquire a momentum in our mind, then it may represent the beginnings of a possible new business opportunity.

From personal experience I have found that an idea of substance—as distinct from a passing thought or fleeting observation—is one that will continue to reoccur and suggest itself over time, one that you will begin to become more confident about and that begins to trigger within you a growing sense of excitement, of challenge, of belief, and even impatience. Once you start to experience these emotions and feelings, you owe it to yourself to elevate the idea from the realm of suggestion and to start subjecting it to some stricter criteria.

The business idea is a starting-point, but no more than that. We must now convince ourselves (and others) that it is a sound business concept: that is, one that can be taken and developed into a successful business venture.

At this point I would like to introduce what I consider to be the single most important ingredient in any business operation, one that I believe must be close to the heart of every entrepreneur, and that is, preoccupation with and commitment to the bottom line. We go into business primarily to make money. If you feel uneasy or uncomfortable about taking that basic principle on board, then don't set up your own business. You may end up running an operation that has the best people, sells the best products, offers the best service, or has the best reputation, but unless that business is making money you are wasting your time. In becoming an entrepreneur you will find that you are having to divide your energies and attention between all aspects of the business. But without doubt, the most important point of focus for any entrepreneur is the bottom line. Everything else must be worked back from that.

So how do you know that the idea you have makes business sense and that it will translate into a profitable and successful enterprise? Obviously there is no way of being absolutely certain about the viability of any operation until you have tried it. But there is an obligation on everyone at this stage of the venture cycle to sit down and to lay out in an honest and realistic way all aspects of the business being proposed. This entails squaring up to and teasing out all the key issues:

- Can I manufacture the product or put together the service, and at what price?

- What markets am I aiming at, what level of demand exists for my product, and what volume of sales can I realistically expect to be able to generate over a five-year period?

- What people and skills resources must I put in place in order to produce, sell, distribute and support my product and to administer my business?

- What type of organisational structure do I need to put in place, and what are the key management functions I need to fill, and with whom?

- What level of investment does the business require, how do I intend raising that finance, and in what way and over what time-scale do I intend repaying the borrowing element?

The main purpose of this exercise is, first of all, to determine for oneself if the basic concept is sound and has potential, and whether the figures add up and suggest beyond reasonable doubt a viable and profitable business. To carry out this appraisal properly you must be prepared to

- devote as much time as is necessary to examine

all aspects of the business in a thorough and comprehensive manner;

- be honest and realistic with yourself regarding the assumptions that you make;

- carry out as much research and seek out whatever advice and assistance you need in order to back up your assumptions and to eliminate or nail down as many of the variables as possible.

I found this preliminary investigation difficult, tiresome, and even frustrating at times. But looking back later I was to discover that the painstaking effort we put into researching, structuring and preparing the operation was to pay handsome dividends. Like a football team facing an important contest, we had prepared ourselves well and left as little as possible to chance. By the time the big day arrived we were very quickly into our stride, getting the business off to a flying start, and experiencing only a minimum of setbacks and surprises, and ended up making a handsome profit in our first year. I firmly believe that an extra six months properly spent on the preparatory stage is worth a full year in business, and it doesn't cost anything as much!

2

Important Attributes

An entrepreneur can be defined as someone who sets out with a sound business idea and then translates it into a viable and successful enterprise. We have already considered the first part of this definition, but the second, "translation" phase represents the most important element and by far the biggest challenge.

So what does it take to be an entrepreneur, and what distinguishes those who set out with a good business idea and succeed in translating it into a profitable business venture? There are, I believe, five key ingredients, which, if properly applied to a sound business concept, will ensure success.

1. Ambition

Every aspiring entrepreneur must have a strong desire to run his or her own business and be filled with a driving ambition to make it work. The reasons for wanting to go it alone are many and will vary in emphasis from person to person; but working for oneself and working for others are very different experiences, and a successful transition from one to the other will entail changes in attitude, outlook, priorities, and values. I don't mean that you should become a different person, but you must be prepared to adopt a more hard-nosed approach to business and be resolute in your determination to achieve your goals. The world of the entrepreneur is one of taking risks, of assuming responsibility, of making tough decisions, of facing stiff competition, and of putting your money where your mouth is. It is not a place for the faint-hearted. You must be ambitious to succeed.

2. Profit Motivation

I have referred earlier to the fact that we go into business primarily to make money and that if you feel shy or uncomfortable about accepting this basic principle, you should not set up your own business. It is time that we in this part of the world started to look at profit and levels of profitability in the same way that they do in the United States and Japan: as the primary justification for private-enterprise investment and the key measurement of business success.

As part of having a healthy bottom line commitment, it is important that we focus on the distinction between sales revenue and profitability. This might appear to be an absurd and unnecessary observation to make, but it is quite extraordinary the number of home-grown businesses I have come across

20

that are revenue-driven and whose energies and efforts are mainly devoted to increasing turnover and becoming bigger players. Signing orders and capturing new customers are only worth celebrating if the resultant revenues will adequately increment the bottom line. There will always be certain business deals that you should be prepared to walk away from and leave to others. At all times have a strong profit orientation.

3. Determination

If there is one single attribute that more than any other represents the hallmark of the successful businessperson I would say it is determination: an absolute resolve to face up to and overcome all the obstacles, difficulties and setbacks that will arise. Don't underestimate the problems you will face in getting your business off the ground, in obtaining the financial backing for a green-field project, in securing the services of top-quality people in a new business venture, in prising open your market and winning customer support for a new and unproven product or service, in relying on suppliers to keep their word and deliver on time. The early stages in particular will be difficult, with one obstacle after another having to be jumped.

I have a vivid personal recollection of spending a long, frustrating year trying to obtain the necessary financial backing for Online Computing. Having put the business plan together, I set off full of confidence and with great naïveté to secure the necessary investment funding. I was adamant from the outset that there were two conditions that would have to be met:

- that the level of funding would be sufficiently generous so as to remove the possibility of any financial pressures arising in our first two years of operation and to allow us to concentrate totally on getting the business off the ground;

- that I would have the majority shareholding in the company and be in a position to run the business in my own way, based on my knowledge of and experience in the computer industry.

I knocked on a large number of financial institutions' doors, only to receive the same response: great idea, great guy, great track record, but come back when you have the necessary collateral and we will be delighted to join you. I approached some prominent businesspeople, who were equally complimentary towards the venture but whose starting position was 51 per cent—minimum—of the equity. I was given lectures on the relative importance of capital versus business expertise and on investor risk versus the risk of the entrepreneur in a new business venture.

My personal finances at that time were not strong. In fact I had no money and was obliged to take out a second mortgage on our house to finance my stake in the company. The last thing I needed was someone telling me that as an investor their risk would be greater than mine and that it should therefore command a higher premium. From where I stood, nothing could be further from the truth. I was putting literally everything on the line: good job, high salary, secure employment, personal reputation—everything, right down to the roof over our heads. The responses I was getting at first unnerved me, then annoyed me, and finally made me more determined than ever to stick to my guns.

So, some fifteen approaches and almost twelve months later, I finally put the project to bed while securing the twin objectives of adequate funding and majority control that I felt were of fundamental importance. It was a good example of what can be achieved through being sufficiently determined. In setting up and developing your own business, never take no for an answer.

4. Business Philosophy

One of the best things we did when setting up Online Computing was to adopt and apply our own distinctive business philosophy. We wanted to set out some key principles that would guide our actions, set standards for our employees, and make us different from, and better than, our competitors. It was simple but very effective, consisting of the following three aims:

(1) to provide the highest standards of customer service and support;

(2) to employ only the best people and adopt a strong work ethic;

(3) to be profit-oriented.

I would advise anyone starting out in business on their own to set down their own clearly defined business philosophy and to embrace it from day 1. Let your business evolve against the background of a clear, distinctive and attractive definition of the way your company intends to conduct its operations. Whatever philosophy you choose, you, the entrepreneur, must adopt it with conviction and communicate it to your staff and to your customers and prospective customers in the market. Wrap it around your products and services; it will provide you with a clear focus and present you with a very effective sales and marketing tool.

5. Professionalism

One of the first problems facing any new business operation is quickly establishing credibility in order to be treated as a serious player. A professional approach will play an important part in helping to bridge that credibility gap and create the confidence and comfort factor needed to get a business momentum going. Because it's a relatively rare commodity it receives a premium rating and can be a significant factor in helping to open the initial doors. When deployed on an on-going basis it will play an important part in developing a strong sense of customer loyalty, enhancing the reputation of the business, and leading to repeat and referral business.

So what is professionalism? Essentially it is a live commitment to doing things properly—as distinct from just doing things. It means being thorough, competent, responsive, reliable, honest and committed in your business dealings. It will manifest itself in a lot of different ways, for example:

- being on time for appointments;

- being properly briefed and prepared before going into meetings;

- investigating thoroughly the customer's requirements;

- presenting your solution and all the relevant information in a comprehensive and concise fashion;

- meeting delivery dates;

- delivering a working product or solution;

- where problems are encountered or are likely to arise, informing the customer early and keeping him or her briefed on progress;

- returning calls;

- running your business efficiently;

- walking away from potential business for which you don't have the resources or the expertise or where the price does not allow you both to do the job properly and make a reasonable profit.

As you can see from some of these examples,

adopting a professional approach doesn't really cost anything, but it can have a significant bearing on helping to get your business off the ground more quickly while giving it a special appeal that can only enhance its future growth and development.

3

The Business Plan

If, having started out with a business concept and after careful consideration and thorough examination of all aspects of the proposed venture, you have reached the conclusion that you have in fact the basis of a sound and viable business operation, then the next step is to lay out all the relevant information in the form of a business plan. In doing so, you should regard this document as having three important functions to fulfil:

(1) to convince you, the promoter, that when all the data pertaining to the proposed venture is set out in a comprehensive and realistic way, it does make sound business sense;

(2) to provide the basis for enabling prospective investors and lenders to assess the viability of the project and measure its opportunity potential;

(3) to form a blueprint for getting the business off the ground and for managing and directing it

through its critical first two years of operation.

In setting out to put together your business plan, there are two important considerations to bear in mind:

- The information pertaining to the business should be comprehensive and detailed, and the figures and assumptions included should be realistic.

- While the plan should be drafted by the promoter, it is advisable to engage the services of an accountant or business consultant in order to properly structure and present the financial aspects of the proposal. However, all input to the preparation of the figures and accounts must come from the promoter and should reflect his or her realistic assumptions both on costs and revenues.

In order to fulfil the objectives stated, the business plan should be divided into a number of main sections, covering (at least) the following elements:

The proposed business

The promoters' background

Market information

Organisational structure and resources

Financial forecasts

Funding requirements

Appendices

Let us now look at what should be contained in each of these sections.

1. The Proposed Business

This should describe in a clear and concise way what the business is all about: the nature of the product or service being proposed, the way in which you believe it is special, and the basis and justification for your belief that an opportunity exists for developing it into a viable and successful business.

2. The Promoters' Background

The background of the promoters is a key element in determining both the prospects and potential for any new business venture. It will come under very close scrutiny from potential investors and lenders, who will want to be satisfied that the promoters

- have the necessary skills and expertise relevant to the proposed business;

- can demonstrate a proven track record in their respective fields;

- represent a balanced team with complementary skills covering the key areas of the business, for example production, sales, management, and finance.

3. Market Information

Many of the projections contained in your business plan will stem from the assumptions you make regarding sales volume and values. It is important, therefore, that you can demonstrate a good knowledge and understanding of your market, set out a sound and realistic sales strategy for tapping into that market, and put forward convincing arguments why you believe you can achieve your revenue projections. Where possible, support your statements with published or private market research reports.

This section should cover all the following areas:

Market description

Market size and growth rate

Main competitors and market shares

Strengths and weaknesses of main competitors

Your own sales and marketing strategy

Perceived advantages and strengths

Why you believe you can attain your revenue targets

4. Organisational Structures and Resources

This section should set out details of the resources required to operate the business in terms of: machinery, staff, accommodation, office equipment, transport, and other facilities. Attention should focus on how best to achieve optimum utilisation of all resources and on keeping costs and investment to an absolute minimum commensurate with meeting the basic requirements of the business. Keep in mind that the initial goal is to get the business up and running and that any extravagance or unnecessary expenditure at the set-up stage cannot be justified and should not be entertained.

Also included in this section should be details of the organisational structure you propose to put in place to ensure the smooth and efficient running of the business. This should cover the key functional operations, such as production, sales, service, finance, and administration. The emphasis should be on implementing simple but clearly defined structures and procedures that will ensure that performance in the key areas of the business can be effectively managed and monitored.

5. Financial Forecasts

This section should set out a summary of the financial projections for the business over a five-year period; the detailed figures and assumptions from which this summary is compiled must be included in an appendix to the proposal. The financial forecasts should include the following data, on a quarterly or annual basis:

Projected sales in units and value

Estimated costs, including both fixed and variable charges

Profit and loss statements

Cash flow projections

Balance sheet

6. Funding Requirements

Having completed the financial forecasts, you will now be in a position to determine the level of funding required to set up and operate the business. I am a great believer in subjecting any business, but most especially a new business, to tight financial disciplines and controls. However, while adopting a policy of operating a lean and efficient operation, it is highly advisable and sensible to seek a level of funding that is higher than that suggested by the financial forecasts, in order to provide you with a comfort factor in the event of delays or unforeseen problems arising during the start-up phase. In other words, adopt a policy of running a tight ship but give yourself the option of being able to tap into additional financial reserves should the need arise. It is far better to have built a contingency factor into your projections at the funding stage than to have to go cap in hand to your backers should things not go exactly to plan. Establishing and retaining credibility with your investors is of paramount importance.

Having decided on an appropriate level of funding, your next step is to determine the best method of securing it, and this is an area where you should engage the services of a competent financial adviser. Generally speaking, where new business ventures are concerned, the necessary funding will come from a combination of the following sources:

Equity investment by the promoters

Equity participation from a third-party source

Bank financing, in the form of overdraft facilities, term loans, or leasing arrangements

The primary objective must be to put in place an

adequate level of funding in line with the needs of the business, but within that you should strive to find an arrangement that

- allows you, the promoter (and your partners), to retain as high a proportion of the equity as possible; this is important for all the obvious reasons, not least the motivation factor;

- secures as much additional equity finance as possible through third-party investors in order to minimise financing costs;

- structures the bank lending element in such a way as to minimise interest charges and allow the maximum leverage in terms of the repayment period.

At the end of the day, the funding package will largely be determined by the perceived viability of your business proposal, by your own credibility and powers of persuasion, and by the prevailing investment climate. It is, however, a vital stage in the whole process and one where I would strongly advocate that you invest as much time, persistence and determination as possible. In setting up your own business you owe it to yourself to put in place the best available financial supports while at the same time securing the maximum returns to you and your partners for your efforts.

7. Appendices

All the necessary back-up information and figures pertaining to the forecasts and assumptions in the main body of the business proposal should be included in a series of appendices. In particular, these should include detailed information on such matters as

Product or service costings

Business overheads

Capital expenditure

Product or service pricing

Sales projections

Credit terms

Lead-time assumptions

Promoters' qualifications, career paths, and achievements

8. Creating the Business Plan

At the beginning of this chapter we reflected on the fact that your business plan would have three important functions to fulfil, one of these being to provide a basis for enabling prospective investors and lenders to assess the viability of the project and measure its potential. Not only should the plan contain all the necessary information for such an assessment, but equally importantly it should be co-ordinated and presented in a logical and concise fashion, so as to be sufficiently interesting to the reader while at the same time doing full justice to your cause. Remember that this document is likely to be the prospective investor's or lender's first exposure to you and your business proposition. While he or she will use its contents to try to establish and measure the viability and potential of the business, they will also be influenced to some extent by the presentation of the case and what that says about you, the promoter, and in particular about your ability to sell yourself and your ideas.

I remember my first attempt at putting together the business plan for Online Computing. Before sending it into circulation I took it to a prominent businessman for his analysis and comments. He virtually took it to pieces and rebuilt it. What came back was a document that was only half the size of the original but that was twice as pertinent and a good deal punchier. So, make sure that the content of your business plan does full justice to your proposal and that its presentation and layout reflect well on you. If report writing is not your forte, then get help in putting the plan together. Remember, this document should represent your passport to funding. Make sure that it is valid, that it incorporates a good picture of yourself, and that it checks out in all important respects. In that way you should ensure a smoother passage and reach your funding destination with a minimum of disruption and delay.

4

Picking the Team

How many times have you heard the saying "It's a people business"? This is particularly applicable to businesses operating in the service sector, but the "people aspect" is extremely important in almost every business situation. For an entrepreneur starting from scratch it is one of the most critical ingredients, and for the following reasons:

● A good entrepreneur will bring many important personal attributes to bear on his or her business: vision, willingness to take risks, a strong driving force, ambition, courage, conviction, new ideas, determination, management and motivation skills, and more. But the extent to which he or she can translate this entrepreneurial spirit into a successful business will depend to a considerable extent on their ability to bring on board the right people. No matter how important you rate what you are bringing to the situation, you must recognise the importance of surrounding yourself with a team of good, carefully chosen people.

- The largest single element of overhead in most company accounts will fall under the heading of salaries and wages. With such a high percentage of your investment going into people, you just cannot afford to make many mistakes, and certainly no serious ones. Team selection, therefore, becomes very important.

So how do you go about picking your team and, even more importantly, ensuring that you choose the right people? To begin with, I would recommend that the question be tackled at two separate levels: partners and staff.

1. Partners

I would strongly advise that every entrepreneur should bring one or more partners into the business with them and give them a slice of the action. This is important for a variety of reasons:

- It enables the entrepreneur's own strengths, skills and expertise to be complemented so as to secure a well-balanced and strong management team.

- The key functions of the business will include production, sales, and finance. It is desirable that responsibility for running these departments be given to highly experienced people with proven track records, and that their motivation levels and commitment to the business be maximised.

- If your key managers have some ownership and partnership involvement in the business it will lessen the temptation to them, and the risks to you, of their being enticed to work for someone else. The better the people, the more important this factor becomes.

- You must not allow yourself to become so stretched or so totally immersed in the day-to-day running of the different parts of the business that you cannot see the wood from the trees. If your company is going to grow and develop, then you will need to devote more of your own time to providing strong leadership, introducing new ideas, and formulating plans and strategies for the on-going expansion of the business.

In choosing those whom you wish to bring in as partners you should set yourself some very strict criteria, as follows:

- Be certain that they have both the skills and the experience that are essential to your business, and that they have proven track records and reputations. The ideal situation is to have people with whom you have already worked and whose suitability and value you can measure. If not, then make sure that they check out with people whose judgement you can trust.

- Only consider people who fully appreciate the difference between having a job and working for themselves: the longer hours, and the greater pressures, risks and responsibilities involved. Ideally they should be people with a strong desire to be self-employed but who do not have your degree of courage and determination to make it happen.

- Where possible, select partners who can easily identify with the principles of strong management and sound business practices and who are able to adopt the bottom-line focus referred to earlier.

A strong, experienced, well-balanced and business-oriented partnership is of fundamental importance, not just in ensuring the success of your business but also in determining the extent of that success in future years. So choose carefully.

2. Staff

Recruiting good staff for a green-field project can be difficult. For most people, job security and present status are naturally important considerations, and they are not going to be easily persuaded to cast them aside and switch to a new business, no matter how exciting and challenging you, the entrepreneur, will view it. So be prepared for some rejections and last-minute changes of heart; but persist in your search for the right people. There are a few observations that are worth making in this regard.

- Your own personal reputation, experience and charisma will be important factors in persuading staff to come on board.

- A young, single person with potential is more likely to be turned on by a new challenge and the prospect of having greater responsibility and freedom of action, and less concerned with, and constrained by, the risk elements.

- Look for people with lots of enthusiasm and energy, who are willing to roll up their sleeves and get stuck in. A new business needs workers, not procrastinators; it needs people who are prepared to work hard and put in long hours, not those brought up in a nine-to-five environment.

- Make contact with industrial training bodies and with third-level colleges, and get them to refer their brightest students to you. We got several of our best people from this source, and they came to us full of enthusiasm and commitment and determined to secure and advance their careers.

Finally, I would recommend that for every appointment you make, the terms and conditions agreed should be formalised and laid out in detail in a letter or contract of employment. This sets the record straight from the outset and avoids the risk of serious misunderstandings arising later on. Remember, your people are your most important asset. Spare no effort in ensuring that you both get and retain the very best.

5

Countdown to Start-up

Having made up your mind to take the plunge, your first reaction will be to chuck in your present job and get on with it. Don't. There will be many preparatory tasks that will have to be undertaken, some of which will have rather longer lead times than you imagined. Many of these can be worked on at evenings and weekends. Only if what you are proposing to do represents a serious conflict of interest with your present employment should you consider resigning your job at the outset.

Either way, your objective should be to get to the starting-blocks with as much of the preparatory work as possible under your belt. So sit down and set out a carefully organised plan of action that identifies all the tasks that will have to be undertaken and the lead times associated with them. Your goal will be to get to a position where your business can be productive from day 1 while incurring the minimum of outlay in getting to that stage.

The following are some of the key functions you will have to address :

43

1. Company Formation

Having decided on a name, you will need to engage a solicitor to form a limited company, register it, and prepare the memorandum and articles of association. Legal processes move slowly, even on mundane tasks; and remember that the bank will require proof of registration before opening a company bank account.

2. Finance

Having agreed a funding package, there will be a good deal of supplementary documentation to be completed before it is finally in place, including:

Shareholders' agreement

Loan guarantees

Leasing agreements

Deeds of assignment

Grant agreements

Bank account authorisations and signatures

3. Accommodation

A suitable premises with enough space to meet your needs over an initial two or three-year period will be required. Depending on the nature of your business, location may be an important consideration and should be borne in mind. Choose accommodation that is functional, meets your basic needs, and does not involve any unnecessary outlay. Only when your business is up and running and making a healthy profit should you consider prestigious accommodation and a more fashionable address. Lease rather than purchase, in order to conserve capital and make it available to the business: investing in a property asset is a luxury that you may be able to afford in the future, but not right now.

Again, bear in mind that having found suitable accommodation you will need to allow at least a further month for the legal end to be tied up.

4. Equipment

In a manufacturing operation the sourcing, ordering, delivery and commissioning of plant and equipment will entail a good deal of planning and preparation and will take time and almost certainly result in some hiccups and delays. Bear this in mind when deciding when to begin operations. Better to have your plant installed and to start payment on your lease than to have staff hanging around with nothing to do and be liable for their wages. Both impact on cash flow, but the second is more damaging to the bottom line and as such is the greater evil.

In a non-manufacturing environment the equipment requirements will usually be minimal and less critical and should be easily handled within the overall lead time to opening day.

Again all items of plant and equipment should, where possible, be leased rather than purchased. It is worth bearing in mind, however, that where equipment is not new, leasing facilities will not normally be available.

5. Suppliers

Where your business involves manufacturing or distribution under a licence, agency or franchise arrangement, you will need to spend some time negotiating the terms of the arrangement, discussing the contract conditions with your solicitor, and ensuring that a formal agreement is in position before setting foot in the market. As a general rule, where important elements of your operation are dependent on sources outside your own control, the terms and conditions governing these relationships need to be nailed down and formalised as early as possible, and certainly before you take any real exposure. Once your business is up and running and relationships with suppliers are cemented, you can rely much more on the trust factor.

6. Sales

This is by far the most important area you will have to address during the preparatory period leading up to opening day. It is imperative that your business be productive from day 1. This means having an order book of some kind in place before you start. So how do you go about achieving that and persuading customers to make the act of faith in you and your new operation? Here are a few suggestions.

- Your original idea and the justification for setting up your new business will have stemmed from your perception of some gap or deficiency or opportunity in a particular market. You will almost certainly have aired and tested your ideas with some key players in that market, and for you to have made the decision to proceed with the venture you will also have had their acknowledgement that there is a need for such a product or service. Now you must seek their active support and persuade them to give you a trial order. Make it as easy as possible for them by minimising their exposure. If necessary, build into the contract guarantees and safeguards in relation to quality, reliability, service, and delivery. After all, if your business is going to succeed then you must be prepared to commit yourself to certain basic performance standards from the outset.

- As someone who has been in business over a number of years and built up a good track record and reputation, you will have had dealings with a lot of companies that believe in you and hold you in high esteem. Now is the time for you to tap this reservoir of goodwill. It is surprising the number of companies whose buying decisions are influenced by personal contact and trust. Obviously the more reputable and reliable you have been in your previous business relationships the stronger your case. So sell yourself and your track record. I can assure you that you will be pleasantly surprised at the level of meaningful support that will be forthcoming from people whom you have looked after well in the past.

- Sit down with your partners and draw up a list of all contacts, friends, relations and neighbours who either directly or indirectly may be in a position to put some initial business your way. Sound out your bank manager, accountant, and solicitor. Where you are representing a major manufacturer or distributor under an agency agreement, you should expect to see at least some referrals from them.

- In considering how to fund your business, we referred to equity participation from a third-party source as being one of the options available. If such a deal could be struck with a potential customer then this would be an ideal means of securing both initial and on-going business. Under such an arrangement there would be a strong incentive for both parties to secure each other's interests.

In conclusion, I would urge you to seek out every source and beat every bush until you have secured enough orders to enable the operation to be productive from the start and provide you with a platform from which you can begin to build the business. As a rough guide, you should aim to have an orders pipeline equivalent to at least 15 per cent of your targeted first-year sales. This level of cover will ensure two things:

- that you are earning a contribution against overheads from the outset, thereby taking the strain off the finances at your most critical stage;

- that you secure a reasonable breathing space for your sales team and thereby make it easier for them to sign up profitable business and meet their first-year targets.

7. Staff

We have already covered the question of staff selection. However, in preparing to launch your business there are three points worth considering regarding the proper utilisation and management of staff.

1. Tailor your people resources precisely to your business volumes. Only take staff on board when you know you are going to have work for them. With a new business in particular, the impact both on finances and on morale of having staff hanging around with little to do will be damaging.

2. Ensure that every person recruited starts out knowing precisely what their responsibilities are, what is expected of them, and who they

report to. At the same time, encourage flexibility of operation in the early days and invite staff to lend a hand whenever and wherever it is most needed.

3. No matter how small the operation or how simple the business, set down on paper an organisation chart. This will ensure that you are clear in your own mind about how you want your business structured and administered; it will also help focus management's attention on what its precise responsibilities are, and allow everybody in the organisation to see what roles they play and where they fit in to the overall scheme of things.

Part 2

Learning to Fly

6

Managing the First Year

The most critical period in the life of any new business is its initial year of operation. What you do, and how you do it, in your first year can either make or break you. A good start will go a long way towards ensuring that your business will be successful. Conversely, serious sins or omissions at this stage will not be easily forgiven, and may be severely punished. So let us home in on this all-important first year of operation.

As an entrepreneur, you are now facing your first major test, that of getting your business off the ground. Your first inclination will probably be to dive in and immerse yourself totally and energetically in all aspects of the operation. But before you do that, I would advise that you stand back momentarily, appraise the targets set out in your business plan, and then define certain goals that you will endeavour to meet in order to secure those business targets. This will result in your starting out with a plan of action that will assist you in organising your activities and help you focus on certain key objectives that will be essential to securing year 1. Such a plan of action should concentrate on the attainment of three main goals:

- Establishing a customer base

- Generating a sales momentum

- Managing and administering the business

Let us consider each of these in turn.

1. Establishing a Customer Base

We referred earlier to the importance of putting an order book in place prior to start-up. The first priority now must be to convert these orders into working products or solutions as quickly as possible. In setting out to achieve this, you must not lose sight of an equally important objective: that of securing a satisfied customer, one who will both continue to spend more money with you and refer other prospective buyers to you. Your first challenge, therefore, will be to balance the immediate priority of the business (shipping product out and getting money in) with the needs of the customer (receiving a quality product on time). This will be more easily achieved if you go about the task in an organised and professional way. The following are some suggestions as to how this might be done.

- Set up a meeting to be attended by both yourself

and your production manager on the one hand and the customer and his or her user or purchasing department on the other. The objective of this meeting will be to review the customer's requirements in detail and ensure that there are no misunderstandings regarding what you are proposing to produce and what the customer is expecting to receive. Confirm the requirements in writing, and have them signed off by both parties.

- Sit in on the initial briefing session between your production manager and his or her team outlining the requirements of the job and determining the resources and time scales required to produce it.

- Meet regularly with your production manager and his or her team to review progress.

- Maintain a personal liaison with the customer, and keep him or her informed of developments. Any problems or setbacks that are likely to result in delays should be communicated to them by you and as early as possible.

- Sit in on the quality control and final testing of the finished product. Insist that all output is subjected to rigorous quality standards prior to shipment.

- On delivery of the product or solution, ensure that the required installation, service and back-up support resources are in place.

- As early as possible, meet with the customer to discuss and review the performance and acceptability level of the finished product or solution.

- Take immediate steps to remedy any problems, defects or deficiencies that may have arisen.

- Obtain the customer's final acceptance.

- Deliver your invoice.

- Collect the payment cheque.

You will notice that I am recommending a significant front-line involvement by the entrepreneur in all aspects of the operation. There will be a time when this will be neither practicable nor desirable; but at this initial stage you must provide the main impetus to ensure that things get done properly and in an organised fashion and on time. Besides, a strong personal involvement by you at this point will be both necessary and beneficial in

- ensuring that those key first orders are properly handled;

- assuring those customers who have put their trust in you at this early stage of your development that you are personally involved and fully committed to looking after their needs;

- setting high standards of performance and service for your own management and staff, to be adhered to from the outset.

The importance of being able to quickly put in place an initial customer base cannot be overstated. Not only will it provide an early kick-start to your operation but it will bring with it some of the essential ingredients that will be required if you are to build the platform from which you can go on to develop your business; for example:

Credibility

One of the main handicaps affecting any new business is that it is very short on credibility: at the outset it is primarily reliant on the reputation, track record and optimism of its promoters. The sooner, therefore, that it can ship product and get satisfied customers onto its books, the sooner it can start generating that all-important credibility factor and begin to be taken seriously.

Reference

There are limits to the amount of business you can generate through your own contacts and reputation. Sooner or later you are going to have to face stiff competition on the open market, where, invariably, prospective buyers will be insisting on having some yardstick by which they can measure your performance. With a couple of good reference sites under your belt your task will be made easier and you can begin to adopt a more confident sales approach.

Revenue

Up until now you will have seen money flowing in one direction only. The sooner you can start to generate a flow of revenue and begin to correct this imbalance, the better. A good start to the financials will work wonders for your confidence and credibility—not to mention the future health and prosperity of the business.

Morale

Remember that your new business venture represents a challenge and is important to all concerned, not least, of course, to your staff. If they see orders flowing in, goods shipping out, invoices being raised, and cheques being banked, it will boost their morale, strengthen their commitment, and contribute enormously to having an industrious work environment. The creation of an early momentum is a tremendous motivating force for all concerned in the business.

2. Generating a Sales Momentum

As an entrepreneur you will quickly learn that in striving to get your business off the ground you will have to be a wearer of many different hats. Perhaps the one you will have the most difficulty in adapting to will be the sales role, unless of course you have had a sales background yourself. Without wishing to cast any aspersions on professional salespeople (I was one myself), it is important to point out that they tend, as a rule, to be assertive, highly optimistic, earnings-motivated, and inclined to do their own thing. In a fully grown, mature business these are admirable qualities to have on your side, but in a newly formed venture, which must learn to crawl before it can walk and walk before it can run, they could spell trouble. So here again you will be faced with the challenge of balancing the needs of the business (getting profitable orders that it can handle) with the needs of the sales force (making sales and maximising earnings). My advice is to lay down certain guidelines governing the operation of the sales role in order to tailor it to the needs and capabilities of the business at this particular juncture:

- Only sell what you can deliver. Do not enter into commitments that you have neither the skills nor the resources to meet.

- Only sign up profitable business. All quotations should be prepared using an agreed estimating and costing system and signed off by management. You will be forced to make some concessions from time to time, but if the price dips below an agreed and acceptable level of profit margin, then walk away and leave it to someone else.

- Concentrate your efforts on pulling in a large number of smaller contracts in preference to a small number of large contracts. These smaller jobs are easier to price, to process, and to extract profit from. For a new company, large contracts could mean greater risks and the danger of creating a deep hole that you may end up spending a lot of time and money digging yourself out of.

Having established these basic guidelines, you must now set about competing for business and getting a sales momentum going. Here again you must be prepared to play a key role yourself and ensure that everything possible is being done to achieve your sales targets. The following are some ideas that you may find useful:

- Once a prospective buyer has been identified, then go along to the initial meeting set up to discuss the proposed requirements. First impressions are vitally important, so make sure you present a positive image of yourself and your company, its capabilities, its business philosophy, and its commitment to its customers. If a prospective buyer is to seriously consider doing business with you, he or she must first be satisfied that they can trust you personally and get a comfortable feeling about your company and the way it conducts its business.

- Bring whatever technical expertise is needed to bear on the situation in order to (*a*) ensure that you fully understand the requirements and can meet them and (*b*) convince the prospective buyer that you have the know-how to both interpret and satisfy his or her needs.

- Prepare a formal proposal that addresses itself to

all the relevant issues that will be of concern to the buyer in arriving at his or her decision.

- Arrange a formal presentation of your proposals to the key executives and personnel in the buyer's organisation. This should preferably be held at your offices, as it gives you the perfect opportunity to expose the key decision-makers to your operation, your people, and your style of doing things. I found in Online Computing that it was this formal presentation that enabled us to make the greatest impact during sales negotiations; and the way in which we used it was a significant factor in influencing decisions and in helping us to get business. (I shall cover this aspect in greater detail in the chapter on sales techniques.)

- Ensure that those customers you have named as references are informed and briefed beforehand, and encourage the prospective buyer to meet with them.

- In the final stages leading up to the decision, maintain regular contact with the prospective buyer, and make yourself available to clear up any outstanding concerns or provide any final assurances.

- On receiving the go-ahead, arrange immediately for a contract to be signed, a deposit invoice submitted, and the deposit cheque collected. The latter is a must, in my view, as (*a*) it is a recognition of the customer's commitment to doing business—more so than any signature on a letter or contract, (*b*) it is an advance contribution towards the cost of producing the product or solution, and (*c*) it is a recognition of your commitment to run your business in a tightly controlled and financially prudent manner.

To this day I have a clear recollection of signing up our very first customer in Online Computing. As a salesman I was pleased to have won the business, but as an entrepreneur I was over the moon with the deposit cheque. Here was our very first customer handing over a cheque to us, and he hadn't even seen what he was going to get for it. Here were we, a brand-new company banking money for something we hadn't yet produced. It was a tremendous tonic, a great morale booster, and our first real indication that we were indeed in business.

I remember walking back to my car and thinking for a moment that perhaps I should hold on to that cheque and have it framed and hung up in the office to commemorate the significance of the occasion. However, by the time I was driving past the first bank my head had regained control from my heart and I popped in and promptly banked it. Thinking back over this event in later years I was surprised that I even considered letting sentiment get in the way of my natural business instinct. Cheques are hard enough to get your hands on at the best of times; when you do, they should not be left hanging around, not even for a few hours, and most certainly not on walls.

3. Managing and Administering the Business

The majority of people who set up their own business will have had some previous exposure to either the production or sales function, and will therefore be able to draw on their earlier experience in setting about generating a sales momentum and putting a customer base in place. However, the overall management of a business is something that many entrepreneurs may have had little or no familiarity with. Whether or not you have had previous management experience, it is a role that you must take on board and assume from day 1. Furthermore, as your business grows and develops, management will become an increasingly more important aspect of your involvement and will take up more of your time.

The effective management of any business will be very dependent on the availability of detailed and up-to-date information regarding its performance. With the major advances that have occurred in microchip technology over the past decade, the tools needed to provide this information are now within the reach of even the smallest business. I would strongly recommend, therefore, that you make provision in your budget for the installation of a personal computer, together with the following standard software packages, which will cater for most of your administration needs over the initial formative phase of your business:

Word-processing

Debtors' ledger

Creditors' ledger

General ledger

Such a system can be put in place for a relatively modest outlay and will provide up-to-the-minute information in relation to the following key areas of your business:

Credit control

Sales performance

Current liabilities

Profit and loss reporting

Balance sheet

A word-processing program will handle all your correspondence needs—letters, reports, sales proposals, specifications, labels, mailing lists, etc.—and in a fraction of the time taken using the typewriter alternative.

While emphasising the need for you to recognise the importance of managing your business from the start, I would suggest that nothing very elaborate will be required during the first year. All you need to put in place is a simple system of management control sufficient to enable you to manage and monitor the business at two separate levels, as follows:

Operational

At this level you are reviewing the day-to-day operational performance of the business.

The vehicle that we used for this in Online Computing was a weekly meeting, held first thing each Monday morning, at which all managers and senior staff attended. We set a time limit of one hour, and only in exceptional circumstances was it allowed to go beyond that. The meeting was structured so as to allow the functional heads to give briefings in respect of the following key areas of operation:

Sales

Production

Customer service

Accounts

Problems were discussed and agreement reached on what action needed to be taken. For example, if the credit controller reported that a particular customer was refusing to pay his or her bill until an outstanding problem was attended to, the matter was referred to customer service, who would take whatever remedial action was necessary and report back the following week. Minutes of the meeting were taken, and circulated to all concerned.

I found these Monday meetings extremely useful. Not only did they keep me in touch with what was going on in the various parts of the business but, equally importantly, they gave everyone else the opportunity to hear what was happening in all other departments.

Financial

At this level you are reviewing the financial performance of the business.

We held monthly board meetings, attended by the partner-directors. The following reports were prepared and issued in advance to each director for consideration and discussion at the board meeting:

Monthly sales report

Report on outstanding debtors' balances

Monthly profit and loss accounts

The main focus of this meeting was our bottom-line performance against budget, both in respect of the previous month and the year to date. Particular attention was paid to sales performance and to the collection of outstanding debts. Our policy from the outset was to run a tight ship, and the monthly board meetings gave us the chance to assess how successful we were in achieving that.

As the business expanded we also began to use these monthly meetings to consider changes in policy and direction and to formulate strategies for the continuing expansion and development of the business.

Summary

In summing up what is required to get off to a good start and to successfully handle that all-important first year, I would emphasise the following points:

- Have a clear vision of what the fundamentals of the business are at this critical juncture, and focus only on them.

- Go about implementing and achieving them in a well-organised and tightly controlled fashion.

- Keep things as simple as possible, and concentrate on one day at a time. The primary objective at this stage is to get the ship afloat and not to send it off on any ambitious or elaborate voyages.

- Make sure that you are running the business and not the other way around. Get into the driver's seat from day 1, and stay there.

7

Sales Techniques

In monitoring the progress of your business, there are a number of key indicators that you will find yourself paying close attention to. Perhaps the most fundamental of these is the level of sales orders booked. If your business is to grow and develop in an orderly and balanced way, then you will need to have an effective sales operation in place: one that ensures a regular flow of business and secures a pipeline of orders sufficient to fuel the needs of the operation.

As a new business striving to get on its feet, you will neither want nor be in a position to afford any extravagant sales jamboree. However, what you must ensure is that your sales effort is aimed in the right directions and has the capability of securing a good hit rate. This will be achieved through adopting an organised sales strategy combined with the deployment of some simple but effective sales techniques.

A successful sales formula must address the two main stages that go to make up a typical sales cycle:

- Prospecting for business

- Negotiating the deal

Let us consider each of these elements in turn.

1. Prospecting for Business

There are many different ways of finding prospective buyers for your products or services, including:

Cold calling

Mail shots

Referrals

Advertising

Promotions

Exhibitions

Seminars

Market research

Most established businesses will put together a marketing plan that will embrace a combination of some or all of the above options. With a new business, you must be economical in the use of your time and resources and seek to channel your efforts into those areas that will be the most cost-effective. For example, it makes little sense for an unknown entity in its first year of operation to spend anything other than a modest amount on advertising, sales promotions, or attendance at trade exhibitions. The immediate priority must be to get out into the market and be prepared to graft hard for those all-important initial contracts. With an established customer base under your belt and a proven reputation you will then be in a much stronger position to market your wares and raise your profile. Until you reach that stage, however, I recommend concentrating your efforts and resources on the following ways of generating prospects:

Cold Calling

Working from trade directories or any other relevant sources, ring around and introduce yourself and your company. Remember, the objective of this call is not to sell anything but rather

- to introduce your product or service;

- to establish whether a need exists (now or at some time in the future);

- where a need does exist, to make an appointment to visit and discuss it; and

- where a need may arise in the future, to write confirming your telephone conversation and your intention to maintain contact.

Aim your call at the highest available level in the organisation, make your contribution as concise and as relevant as possible, and above all adopt a friendly and relaxed tone. After all, if the person concerned is a potential user, you should be making it as easy as possible for him or her to agree to meet with you.

Mail Shots

Compile a data-base of prospective users on your computer system, and continue to update it as your information sources and market research expand. Using your word-processor you can then implement a mailing system to circulate standard introductory letters or to tailor your communication to the specific needs of different companies, markets, and market sectors. Follow up each letter with a telephone call aimed at determining whether a need exists and, where it does, securing an appointment to discuss.

Referrals

Cultivate the habit of encouraging your customers, prospective customers, suppliers, advisers, friends and acquaintances, relatives, neighbours and all other contacts to refer you to potential buyers. This is perhaps the most fertile and effective source for new business during your formative years. In particular, I have found from experience that a satisfied customer will be only too happy to recommend you and to spread the word on your behalf.

2. Negotiating the Deal

As an entrepreneur striving to get your business established, you must endeavour to implement an organised, clearly focused and economical sales strategy. Resist the temptation to shoot at everything that moves. This is not only wasteful in terms of resources but will also lead to a good deal of frustration and be damaging to morale. A good salesperson is one who qualifies their leads, concentrates their efforts on those prospects whose requirements they are best qualified to meet, and secures a high hit rate.

So how do we set about persuading a prospective buyer whose business we want, to agree to do business with us? I have a personal selling philosophy that has been developed and used over many years and that has proved to be very effective. I set it out below in the hope that it may be of some assistance to you in your efforts to optimise sales performance.

At the outset you must recognise that if you are to make any given sale, then the prospective buyer must be satisfied on three fundamental issues:

- that they can trust you personally;

- that they have confidence in the ability of your company to do the job;

- that what you are proposing meets their needs and satisfies their main buying criteria.

If you are unable to deliver on all three of these

elements, then your chances of securing a deal will be very slim indeed. So let us examine a typical sales negotiation and see how it can best be orchestrated to secure these essential criteria. To do this—and at the risk of oversimplifying the process—I am going to break the sales cycle down into seven separate phases, as follows:

Initial meeting

Establishing the requirements

Preparing the sales proposal

Making a sales presentation

Using your references

Reviewing the state of play

Recovering lost ground

1. Initial Meeting

Your main function at this initial meeting should be to listen. Don't go in shooting from the hip; in fact keep the powder absolutely dry until you have a picture of what the target is that you're expected to aim at. Your first objective must be to extract the following basic information from the prospective customer:

- a brief description of their business;

- an outline of their requirements, including expected delivery dates;

- an indication of how much they are budgeting to spend;

- which other suppliers they are having discussions with;

- what (in order of priority) the main considerations are that will influence the choice of supplier;

- what the decision-making process will consist of and who the key people are who will influence the decision;

- what timetable they are working to;

- whether there is any other relevant information that you should know about.

Having obtained this information, you should now formulate an initial response, tailoring it as much as possible to the requirements as outlined. This should not be a "hard sell" but rather a relaxed presentation aimed at creating a good first impression of yourself and your company and its ability to handle the requirements. You should cover the following:

- your own personal background and track record;

- a brief profile of your company;

- a summary of your business philosophy;

- why you believe you are equipped and suited to meet the requirements, highlighting, where appropriate, similar situations that you have been involved in;

- how you propose to handle the negotiations and what specific next steps you propose to take.

If you can come away from this initial meeting with sufficient information to enable you to formulate a sales strategy while leaving behind you a good first impression, then you will have made a solid start and cleared that first important hurdle.

2. Establishing the Requirements

The next step is to take whatever actions are necessary in order to establish a clear understanding of the prospective customer's needs. This will entail having your production, technical and support personnel examine the requirements and discuss them in detail with the purchaser. From this should emerge a precise definition of the product or service being sought. Ideally this should be documented and submitted for approval. Where a specification has already been provided, any points of clarification or elaboration emerging from your discussions should be detailed and approved. The thoroughness and professionalism of your approach to the examination of the customer's requirements can have an important bearing on their perception of how you would ultimately perform should you be awarded the contract.

3. Preparing the Sales Proposal

I have always adopted the principle that no two sales situations are ever exactly the same. You may be asked to supply a standard product or service, but the selection criteria will vary in both content and emphasis from one situation to the next. It is important, therefore, to examine carefully all the information obtained during your initial meeting and to formulate a response that is tailored to the specific demands and expectations as outlined. The list (in order of priority) of main considerations that will influence the choice of supplier should be used to determine the shape and emphasis of your sales proposal and presentation. In particular, you should address each of the criteria set and show how and to what extent you propose to meet them.

The sales proposal itself should be both relevant and concise and should cover the following main areas:

Proposal summary

Details of what it is you are proposing to supply

Cost details

Profile of your company

List of reference sites, giving contact names and telephone numbers

Advantages of your proposal

Brief profile of the main members of your staff who will be associated with the project

All detailed technical or other back-up data should be included at the back of the report, or submitted as a separate document. The objective should be to make the sales proposal itself as readable and as agreeable as possible.

When all submissions have been received and given some initial consideration, you should arrange a meeting with the prospective buyer to review your proposal and to ascertain the following:

- how it measures up to the stated requirements and criteria set;

- what the advantages and disadvantages of your proposal are as the customer perceives them;

- how it compares with the other submissions received.

You will now be in a position to review your

proposals and make whatever revisions in content or in emphasis that may be necessary as part of your formal sales presentation.

4. Making a Sales Presentation

Arrange to make a formal presentation of your proposals to the relevant executives and personnel from the buyer's organisation. This should preferably be held at your own offices and should be aimed in particular at the key people who will influence the buying decision. I referred earlier to the fact that in Online Computing we used this gathering to good effect and found that it had a significant impact on the outcome of many important sales negotiations. We tended to use a standard agenda, which consisted of the following main elements.

1.   On arrival we would bring the visitors on a tour of the premises, allowing them the opportunity to see our facilities, meet some of our people, and get a feel for the general atmosphere and work environment. In particular we would highlight what we considered to be important support aspects, such as our customer training facilities and customer services unit.

2.   The presentation itself would be done with the aid of an overhead projector and flip-charts and would be divided into three main parts.

3. In part 1 we gave an overview of the company and its achievements, outlined its philosophy and way of doing business, and profiled some of our main customers. The objective of this part of the presentation was to register a high level of credibility for our company.

4. In part 2 the production director outlined the way in which we would propose to handle the buyer's requirements and what resources and facilities we had at our disposal to carry out that task. This would be followed by a demonstration of what we could offer, simulating as much as possible of the buyer's specific needs. The objective of this part of the presentation was to register our competence in understanding and being able to deliver what was required.

5. In part 3 the customer services director set out details of the training and back-up services we operated and how we would propose to support both the prospective customer and the products being proposed on an on-going basis. The objective of this part of the presentation was to demonstrate our commitment to after-sales service and on-going customer support.

6. The presentation was then wrapped up with a question-and-answer session, allowing the buyer the opportunity to clarify any outstanding issues while enabling us to determine how we were measuring up in relation to the criteria set.

5. Using Your References

The best salesperson you could possibly have is a happy customer. What he or she has to say about your products and services will have a greater impact on a prospective buyer than anything you will have said on your own behalf. Now, at this critical stage of the sales negotiation, when your proposal is being given serious consideration, the purchaser will want to be reassured that the decision he or she is about to make is the correct one. A satisfied customer with a positive story to tell is exactly what you both now need; so make good use of your customer references.

6. Reviewing the State of Play

Having done all the hard work associated with the preparation and presentation of your proposal, there is a natural tendency to sit back and wait for the order. Don't. The final phase of any sales negotiation is critical, and fraught with danger. I have been at the receiving end of enough situations where intended recommendations have been changed, and even decisions reversed, to know that you must keep riding out until you have passed the winning-post. So use any excuse you can find to keep in contact with the prospective buyer. If you have established a good personal relationship during the period of negotiation, then he or she will almost certainly be willing to mark your card and let you know the state of play. And when you do get the nod, then collect the deposit cheque and get a contract signed without delay.

I remember us learning a very hard lesson on the importance of quickly securing the customer's go-ahead in writing and of the dangers involved in being lulled into a false sense of security on the back of purely verbal declarations of intent, no matter how well-intentioned these might appear to be. We had developed a stud farm management system, which was installed and was operating very successfully in one of Europe's best-known stud farms. This system was generating a good deal of interest within the bloodstock industry generally, and we were having meetings and presentations with quite a number of other potential buyers.

Our discussions with one particular stud farm had reached an advanced stage; we had agreed the terms of a deal with them, and the local stud farm manager had indicated his intention to proceed with us. This particular farm was owned by an internationally famous multi-millionaire who lived in the heart of the bloodstock belt on the east coast of America. He extended an invitation to us to visit him at his headquarters in the States and to discuss with him how the system we were proposing to install at his European farm could be adapted and utilised to handle his extensive breeding interests in America. Naturally we didn't need much encouragement to take up that offer and lost no time in getting ourselves off to Washington.

On the morning of the appointment a chauffeur-driven stretch limousine arrived at our hotel to pick us up and whisk us off through the beautiful countryside of Virginia to this truly magnificent home set at the edge of a bloodstock centre that extended across thousands of acres of farmland. I remember thinking at the time that this place made even Southfork look ordinary. On arrival we were warmly greeted by the owner and taken to his study, where we spent several hours discussing and agreeing the details of the proposed stud farm management system. Afterwards he introduced us to members of his family and staff, and then took us on a guided tour of the farm, proudly showing off his most valuable stallions, many of which were winners of some of the biggest prize money on race-tracks throughout America, Europe, and Japan. To cap it all he then told us he was putting his chauffeur at our disposal for the remainder of the day so that we could see as much of Washington as we wished. We said our farewells, climbed into the back of the limo, and instructed the driver to take us to the White House, Capitol Hill, the Pentagon, and Arlington National Cemetery. On the journey back to Washington, I remember stretching out in the back of the limousine and commenting to my colleague that this was the only way to do business.

Later that evening, when we arrived back at our hotel, I rang the office in Dublin to inform them of our "success." As far as I was concerned the deal was in the bag, so much so that I allowed a further two weeks to elapse before renewing contact with the stud farm's European management. When I did I got the shock of my life: the contract had just been awarded to IBM. I was numbed, outraged, and furious with the person concerned, who, less than a month earlier, had declared his intention to do business with us.

Of course, once I calmed down and reflected

properly on the situation I realised that I had only myself to blame for what had happened. Verbal declarations of intent, invitations to Washington, chauffeurs and stretch limos are all very good for the ego but they are no substitute for a signed contract. I had taken my eye off the ball and allowed IBM to slip in and pinch the business right from under my nose. And when it comes to the art of selling and the essentials of good business practice, they don't come any better than IBM. I resolved that I would never again allow the go-ahead from a prospective buyer to hang in mid-air for a moment longer than was necessary without quickly converting it into a signed formal agreement. Remember that in a competitive business environment, everyone is hungry for business. You can never afford to relax your guard.

7. Recovering Lost Ground

If during the course of any sales cycle you have reason to believe that you are losing ground and are falling behind in the race, then you will obviously want to reappraise the situation, and you may wish to take corrective action. In order to make an informed decision on this and to enable you to take effective and meaningful steps to retrieve the situation (should you decide to do so), the following questions should be addressed:

●   Is your relationship with the prospective buyer sufficiently close to allow you to establish whether the matter is genuinely a lost cause and beyond recovery, and if so for what reasons?

- Where it is recoverable, can you determine what those factors are that need to be dealt with and in what way your original proposal needs to be modified if the matter is to be redressed?

- Having established what needs to be done to put you back into serious contention, are you (*a*) able to meet the criteria set and (*b*) prepared to do so while at the same time ensuring that your own business interests are being safeguarded?

In general I would take the view that if a contract is worth having, you should be prepared to fight hard to get it; the fact that you may sometimes have to come from off the pace should not deter you. The most important issue to be considered is whether the sale is going to add an acceptable level of value to your business. If it does, then go for it and don't let anything stand in your way.

We had many instances in Online Computing where we had to overcome obstacles of varying heights on different occasions before we could secure the contract. The one I remember most vividly involved the Irish subsidiary of a large American corporation with which we were already doing business. The customer concerned was a pleasure to deal with, in the sense that he knew exactly what he wanted, communicated his requirements clearly, only implemented systems that were relevant and that enhanced the performance of his operation, appreciated being looked after properly, and always put his cheque in the post.

We got a call from him one day to say that the parent company in America had taken a corporate decision to standardise on one particular make of computer hardware for use throughout all its subsidiaries worldwide, and, as that was not the make we supplied, then our system would have to be replaced. Because of the excellent working relationship between us, the news came as a bitter blow—both to him and his team as well as to Online. For us, apart from the immediate financial loss, there would also be a considerable amount of additional extension business that we would miss out on, and in any event customers as good as this one were in short supply.

So, having considered the implications of the news, we decided that we would immediately set about trying to retrieve the situation. We requested permission to address all the relevant senior executives at the company's corporate headquarters, booked our plane tickets to Boston, and sat down to plan and prepare our presentation.

On the plus side, we knew that we were held in high esteem by the Irish subsidiary and that our products and standards of service had been tested and proven. On the negative side, we had to accept that we could not supply the make of computer now being introduced throughout the company. We knew, therefore, that if we were to stand any chance of winning we would have to come up with a solution that would mitigate the impact of this and not leave the company any worse off in terms of being able to exchange data between its various subsidiaries and with head office. We were in fact able to come up with modifications to our own system to enable it to talk freely to the other make of computer, thereby making the differences between them transparent to the user.

Our presentation in the States was well received by the management there, and they gave approval for their Irish subsidiary to remain with us. Their decision was influenced by three factors in particular:

- our ability to neutralise the differences between the two makes of computer in those areas where it mattered to them;

- our determination to meet their senior management to present our case and our willingness to cross the Atlantic to do so;

- our reputation and service record to date and the strong references and recommendations made on our behalf by the Irish subsidiary.

So, if you have to recover lost ground in a sales situation you can certainly do so, provided that

(1) you can identify the main reasons for having fallen behind;

(2) you are able to address those reasons and either eliminate or find a way around them;

(3) you press home your plus points and draw heavily on your customer references for support; and

(4) you are prepared to go into overdrive and really get stuck in.

However, the questions you must first ask yourself are: do I really want this contract; is it my kind of business; and will it adequately increment the bottom line? At the end of the day, if the business is worth having, then it is worth fighting for.

8

Servicing the Customer

Look after the customer and the business will look after itself. That may be an oversimplification of the process, but the sentiment it expresses is of fundamental importance and must be fully recognised by every entrepreneur who is committed to staying the course. Customers generate revenue; revenue generates profit; profit generates a healthy business; and a healthy business generates secure jobs. Everyone in the company must be made aware of that simple equation. The customer pays the bills, so in every business production he or she must be centre stage, and their lead role should be acknowledged and given the attention that it deserves.

I came from an industry that for a long time had things pretty much its own way. It was a seller's market, and there was so much business to be had that there was a tendency to focus more on the beauty of the technology rather than on the true needs and entitlements of the customer. The computer industry has bred more than its share of technocrats, people who are exceptionally bright but whose preoccupation with the hardware tended to make them somewhat aloof and removed from the real, practical needs of the businesspeople they were meant to be serving.

In recent years the business world has begun to reappraise its investment in computer technology and to examine more closely the performance and suitability of its installed systems. Emerging now is a much more perceptive, more conservative and more demanding purchaser, who is intent on installing cost-effective solutions and getting real value for money. For the first time in its history the computer industry is having to adapt to a much harsher business climate—one where the user is now calling the shots and dictating the state of play. This, of course, is as it should be. In business you undervalue the role and importance of the customer at your peril.

I referred earlier to the fact that in Online Computing we adopted and applied our own distinctive business philosophy. A key element in this philosophy was our commitment to providing the highest standards of customer service and support. I am fully convinced that one of the main reasons we got off the ground so quickly and developed our business so easily was the reputation we enjoyed for looking after our customers. Everyone in the company, from top to bottom, was service-oriented. The customer was central to all our activities and the main focus of our attentions. It was a policy that was to pay rich dividends, and one that I would recommend every entrepreneur to adopt as his or her signature tune.

There are many different ingredients that go to make up a healthy customer service environment. The following are some that are worth considering.

1. Customer Awareness

Use every opportunity to promote a culture of service and customer awareness throughout your organisation. Make it a central part of your staff training and development programmes. Let it manifest itself in a variety of ways, from simply being courteous, friendly and helpful in your ordinary everyday dealings with your customers to being responsive to their needs and problems as they arise. Everybody in the company, from the receptionist to the managing director, has a part to play in contributing to this customer-friendly environment. A customer is like every other human being: he or she likes to feel needed and enjoys being made to feel important. Do it and you are creating just the right environment for a sound and lasting business relationship.

2. High Standards

The customer is entitled to expect the best and to get it. Commit yourself to running a business that performs to the highest standards of excellence. Implement rigorous quality control and product testing procedures to ensure that you only deliver quality goods and services. Invite your customers to appraise your performance level, and use the feedback to review your method of operation and to make changes to it where necessary. Here again, everybody in the company has a part to play in the attainment of high standards of performance; so set those standards for all parts of the operation, and do it from day 1. If staff get used to running a sloppy show, it will be much more difficult to remedy this later.

3. Customer Training

In Online Computing we had a strong attachment to the concept of customer training. We had our own training room, which was fitted out with desks, video equipment, monitors, overhead projector, flip-chart, and a library of training videos. Our attitude in delivering a product or solution was that the customer should be properly trained prior to its arrival, so as to make the transition as smooth and as painless as possible. We ran formal training courses involving all the relevant customer staff, aimed at familiarising them both with computers in general and with the use and application of their own systems in particular. We found this method of training to be very beneficial, both to our customers and to ourselves, in that

- it brought both parties together at an early stage in the relationship and led to good co-operation and team work and to the elimination of the "them and us" syndrome;

- it made for a much smoother transition process and minimised the hostility factor that is often associated with the introduction of new systems and procedures; and

- it meant that the customer became self-sufficient

much sooner and was therefore less dependent on the services of our support personnel.

Not every business will either need or benefit from the type of training programmes we adopted. But where possible, I would be exercising the imagination to come up with some equivalent or alternative arrangement that would be similarly helpful in winning the confidence of the customer and establishing close co-operation and a strong partnership as early in the relationship as possible.

4. Customer Services Unit

Within every organisation the engine-room for the provision of support services should be a customer services unit. This should be staffed by competent personnel who are properly trained in the use of your products and services, who have good communication skills, and who are equipped to provide a full range of support services to customers throughout all stages of the business relationship:

● providing on-the-spot assistance and support during the delivery and installation phase, and

● providing advice and back-up support as required on an on-going basis.

Your reputation for service will stand or fall on the quality of the performance of your customer services unit. Keep it under regular review to ensure that it is meeting customers' needs and that it is receiving full backing and support both from you and your management team.

5. Management Accessibility

We have already referred to the fact that everyone in the company has a part to play in generating a healthy customer service environment. Management in particular have a key role to play, both in terms of setting the standards and in leading by example.

Generally speaking, where a business arrangement is progressing according to plan, the customer will be quite happy to deal with those members of your staff who are assigned to the project. However, when problems or difficulties arise and the customer begins to feel worried and exposed, then he or she is going to come looking for you or for one of your partners, seeking reassurance that the matter will be dealt with and remedied. This is the point at which a customer is likely to feel most vulnerable, and they are going to feel an awful lot worse if they have difficulty in gaining access to someone in authority.

Conversely, if you make yourself readily available to listen to the customer's problem, investigate the reasons for it, get back to them to confirm what actions are being taken to correct the situation, and keep them informed on how the matter is progressing, then you will have gone a long way towards restoring their confidence. Similarly, where you encounter unforeseen problems at the production stage that are likely to lead to delivery delays or to other changes in arrangements, then notify the customer immediately rather than let the matter lie and have them receive a nasty surprise later.

It is much easier to handle customer disappointment if you are seen to be taking the initiative and are being honest and above-board on the matter. Every business, no matter how efficiently it is run, will encounter problems and difficulties from time to time. It is how you handle them, and their impact on the customer, that is important. Both you and your partners have a primary responsibility in this regard.

9

Accounting for Your Business

So far so good. Your business is up and running. Things are beginning to fall into place. The operation is starting to hum. Morale is high. Everyone is busy. Customers are happy, and willing to proclaim how well they have been looked after. But are you really running a successful operation?

Well, the only meaningful measurement of business success will be the condition of your bottom line. It is fine to have a good team, an efficient operation, loyal customers, and a good reputation, but if the first essential ingredient is missing then you, the entrepreneur, will not have achieved your fundamental goal. At the end of the day, business is all about profits and levels of profitability; it's about wealth creation. The returns from your operation must adequately reflect the level of investment made, the degree of risk taken, and what has been put into it in terms of blood, sweat, and tears. In my view no entrepreneur should ever feel coy or be taken to task about making money. He or she should see to it that they do, and be applauded for so doing. We need all the entrepreneurial vocations we can get.

In securing the health of the patient there are some basic administrative procedures that you must make sure are in place and are functioning properly.

1. Pricing

In very basic terms, the price at which you sell your product or service must reflect both the cost of production and a mark-up factor that is sufficient to cover all the running costs of the business while leaving you with a margin of profit that will ensure an adequate return on the investment.

In a typical service industry, pricing will be a relatively straightforward exercise, while in certain manufacturing operations it could be much more complex. Similarly, certain operations will be more prone to price volatility than others, particularly those exposed to fluctuating raw material prices and currency exchange rates. In every business, prices should be calculated not on a "seat of the pants" basis but in accordance with a predetermined costing and estimating formula that takes proper account of the different parameters that are relevant to your own particular business. If necessary, seek the advice and assistance of your accountant in putting together an accurate costing system.

Having established a reliable pricing formula, you will now need to keep it under regular review in order to reflect changes to the input parameters. In any event you will need to revise prices on an annual basis (at least) to reflect increases in your level of overheads. Such price increases should be in line with inflation and with increases in the cost of living index, and should be formally notified in writing to customers in advance of their take-effect date.

2. Billing

A good billing system is one that

- picks up and assembles all the relevant charges in accordance with the terms of the contract, and

- ensures the arrival of the invoice at the customer's premises hot on the heels of the goods or services supplied.

The key to a good billing system is to keep it as simple and as foolproof as possible. In theory, it should not be possible for goods or services to leave your premises without the corresponding invoice being raised containing all of the agreed charges. But in practice this sometimes happens, especially where internal systems are too loose or where checks and audits are inadequate. So put a billing procedure in place that is simple but effective, and get your accountant to vet it and to suggest ways in which it can be cross-checked to ensure that it is as watertight as possible. And insist as a matter of company policy that the invoice is always issued immediately after despatch of the goods or services.

3. Credit Control

In Online Computing we operated a very stringent policy of credit control. Our rationale for that was very simple. We worked extremely hard to ensure that our customers received quality products and solutions, backed up with the highest standards of service and support. We were prepared, if necessary, to stand on our head for our customers. Now, having delivered the goods, we expected them to look after us.

Our official credit terms were seven days from date of delivery of invoice, and while we didn't always achieve that, we were extremely persistent in chasing all outstanding amounts. As a result we generated a consistently strong cash flow and managed to keep our level of debtors at an absolute minimum. We were also motivated by the fact that when we first started in business, in the late 1970s, interest rates were extremely high: a bank overdraft at 18 per cent was a luxury we could do without. It didn't take a financial genius to work out that the difference between having money in our bank account rather than in the customer's was almost as important as the margin on the products and services we were providing.

The job of credit controller in any business is a difficult but vitally important one. The conventional approach has been to send out monthly statements and wait for the cheques to arrive. In reality it doesn't work like that, except in a minority of cases. By all means send out your statements, but follow them up with telephone calls to remind customers that there is a payment due. If necessary, make arrangements to have a cheque collected. Be as persistent as you need to be, but get the money in.

Everybody in business is slow to part with money; in a majority of cases they will want to leave it for as long as they can, and that is very understandable from their point of view. But you have your own business and its interests to consider, and nobody else is going to do that for you. And remember that generating profitable business is not of itself a guarantee that you will survive in business. Cash flow is the essential fuel needed to keep the engine running on a day-to-day basis. If there is not enough of that in the tank, you will be forced to stop—no matter how good the condition of the engine or how smart you thought the car looked.

Another important advantage of running a policy of tight credit control is that it minimises the risk of being at the receiving end of a bad debt. We had a good lesson in this regard in the first six months of our existence. It was one of the first batch of contracts we had signed up, and involved a six-figure sum. On signature of the contract we asked for, and received, a deposit—equivalent to 25 per cent of the value of the deal. On delivery of the hardware and software we requested payment of the balance within seven days. We received most of it, except for a couple of thousand pounds that was retained pending performance of the system.

Less than three weeks later the company concerned was in financial difficulty. We recovered the balance by removing some computer terminals equivalent to the amount owed. But it was a very close shave. If we had not been pursuing such a stringent policy of credit control we would have taken a big hit in our first six months of operation—one that we might not have been able to recover from. It was a salutary lesson, and one that we were never to forget.

4. Profit and Loss Accounts

As an entrepreneur, it is a good self-discipline to get into the habit from the very outset of accounting for your stewardship on a regular basis. All the data you need to assess and monitor the performance of your business will be contained in the monthly profit and loss accounts. These will provide you with all the key indicators—sales, cost of sales, gross margins, running costs, and net profit or loss—both in respect of the previous month and the year to date, and with comparisons against the forecasts for the current year and against the actuals for the year before.

As we saw in an earlier chapter, the forum for reviewing the financial performance of the business should be a monthly board meeting attended by at least all the executive directors. Analyse and discuss the accounts, and identify those areas where your performance is not in accordance with expectations and where action needs to be taken. If there are fundamental or persistent problems staring out from under those figures, then face up to them and do whatever is needed to resolve them; they will not go away. The sooner you address any difficulties you may have and take whatever actions are required, the better. In doing so you will discover that to be successful in business you must be prepared to face up to making hard choices and taking difficult decisions.

Any entrepreneur who tries to be all things to all people is heading for trouble. If you thought that by going into business you were entering a popularity stakes, you were sorely misguided. The world of business is exciting and fulfilling, but it is certainly no beauty contest.

5. Bank Manager

I would strongly recommend that you develop a good working relationship with your bank manager. You need him or her on your side, not just now but in the future when you will be seeking additional funding to finance the expansion and continuing development of your business. So cultivate the bank manager and build up a store of brownie points.

Don't wait for the bank to contact you to find out what is going on: send them a copy of your quarterly accounts, with a one-page summary of the state of play. If there are some hiccups along the way, keep the bank informed—particularly if these are likely to result in your borrowing arrangements being stretched or temporarily breached. As with your customers, if the bank manager is put in the picture early regarding a problem or difficulty that has arisen, he or she is likely to be more understanding and accommodating in helping to find a solution.

When your annual audited accounts are finalised,

the bank will require a copy. Use the opportunity to get the bank manager to visit, and let him or her see at first hand how things are going. Take them to lunch; if your results are good you will almost certainly see them picking up the tab. Everyone loves a winner!

10

The Outside World

Anybody reading this book up to this point could be forgiven for thinking that a successful entrepreneur is someone who eats, sleeps and drinks his or her business to the exclusion of everything and everybody else. I have come across a number of instances where this is so, but it is not a course of action I would ever prescribe. As with everything else in life, we should try to achieve a proper balance and harmony between our work responsibilities and our other interests and pursuits. While maintaining our commitment to running a successful business we should at the same time be capable of enjoying a sensible relationship with the outside world. The two are not mutually exclusive.

The most common manifestations of what I would describe as the "married to the business" malady are:

- A tendency to think that the more hours you put into the business the more successful it will be. This is true up to a point, but, like everything else, the law of diminishing returns will eventually set in. Overwork will almost certainly lead to strains and stresses, both within and outside of the business.

- Not appreciating the importance of being organised and of planning your work load and managing your time more efficiently. A disorganised approach to work will inevitably lead to your staying on late at night or coming back in to the office at weekends to compensate for the time lost.

- An inadequate diet of leisure and relaxation pursuits, which are essential to the health and well-being of both the mind and body. You may genuinely not have the time to play regular rounds of golf or spend afternoons at the races, but there are countless other forms of relaxation that are not as demanding on your time but just as valuable in producing a clear mind and a healthy body.

The following are some simple guidelines that may be helpful in ensuring that you achieve a reasonable balance between work and play.

- Sit down for a few minutes at the beginning of each day or each week and organise and plan your work schedule.

- Make sure you take enough time off each week to relax and be with your family and friends.

- Make it a rule to spend a certain amount of time each week engaged in some form of exercise activity, whether it be walking, jogging, swimming, tennis, squash, or whatever turns you on.

● Go away on holiday at least once a year, just to get completely detached from it all for a couple of weeks.

You owe it to yourself and to your business to allocate some portion of your time schedule to relaxation and leisure pursuits. Remember, there are graveyards everywhere full of indispensable people. And whereas one of the reasons we go into business on our own is to make money, just make sure that in your hurry to do so you don't end up leaving it all after you.

Part 3

Handling Heights

11

Moving Up a Gear

There are three readily identifiable stages in the development of any new business:

(1)   getting the business off the ground;

(2)   consolidating the business in its basic form and getting it firmly established on solid foundations;

(3)   developing and expanding the business and embarking on a growth phase.

As a rough guide, the first stage will take at least two years, followed by a further year of consolidation. Only when you are satisfied that you have firmly established the business in its original or basic form should you consider going for growth. Having successfully accomplished the most difficult part, it would be absolute madness if you were now to get carried away and start shooting for the stars before you have properly anchored the basic business.

Yet there is inherent in the make-up of most

entrepreneurs a degree of impatience with the status quo, and an urgency and a thirst for new challenges and for breaking new ground. I have known several dynamic entrepreneurs who, filled with good ideas and a strong visionary sense, have opened many new doors and put ambitious plans in place and then moved on too quickly to the next challenge before putting enough flesh on the original framework, only to see it buckle and collapse around them. The natural urgency and drive of the entrepreneur must be tempered with a degree of patience and self-discipline in order to properly pace the development of the business and ensure that it has sufficient nourishment and muscle to be able to look after itself and enjoy a long and healthy life-span.

So how can you be sure that you have successfully completed stages 1 and 2 and are now ready to increase the tempo and embark on an expansionary phase? Many of the signs will be fairly obvious, and will certainly include most or all of the following:

- A solid base of loyal customers who are paying their bills on time and who are readily prepared to endorse your company and its products.

- An increasing level of new and repeat business and a feeling that those sales are more plentiful and are becoming easier to achieve.

- A greater awareness in the market of your presence and a growing recognition of your strengths and of the attractions and benefits of doing business with you.

- A profitable bottom line, representing an acceptable return on investment and reflecting an inherently sound and healthy business operation.

- A strong cash flow position and a steadily diminishing and manageable level of indebtedness.

- An organisation that is functioning smoothly and efficiently in all the key areas of the business: production, sales, finance, and administration.

- An easier ride when it comes to recruiting new staff, and an increasing level of interest in your company from qualified and experienced personnel.

- A growing feeling of confidence throughout the company, but most particularly on your own part.

- An awareness of the necessity for you to become less engrossed in the day-to-day running of the business and more involved with planning and strategic issues and with growth management.

Standing back from the day-to-day issues in order to take a longer-term view of the business is essential. As a maturing businessperson you must get into the habit of reviewing your operations and visualising where your revenues will come from in the future and how they will be generated. One thing is certain: your business, if it is to be successful over time, must be market-driven. Remember, it is what the customer wants that matters, and his or her needs, tastes and preferences will be changing constantly.

Don't be lulled into any false sense of security just because things happen to be going well right now. Your satisfaction and pride in your products or services may be well justified, but remember that today's business world is characterised by changing markets and intense competition. To be successful in the medium to long term you must be willing to adapt and change your existing business, to develop or acquire new products and services, to expand into new markets and market sectors, and, where necessary, to diversify into new but preferably complementary areas of operation.

Strategy Formulation

In just the same way as, when starting out to set up your business, you embarked on a detailed and comprehensive investigation and preparation process, a similar approach should now be adopted in formulating an effective company strategy for its future development and expansion. An increasing proportion of your monthly board meetings should be devoted to the discussion of new plans, objectives and strategies to secure the continued growth and enhancement of the business.

One approach would be to set up a small but specially chosen strategy formulation group, whose brief would be to investigate and report in detail on a range of options emanating from discussions held at board level. This group would then be responsible for reporting back to the full board for further consideration of the various issues raised and for recommendations to be made and decisions taken. An important aspect of this process will be establishing a proper balance between ensuring that the normal day-to-day work of the company can continue uninterrupted while at the same time guaranteeing that enough thought, planning, effort and resources are being applied to considering and securing its future growth and development.

The result of these deliberations should be a business proposal, laid out in much the same way as the original proposal used to get the company established. You may now have three or more years of running a business under your belt and be tempted to cut corners the second time around. Don't. In business, adhering to certain basic standards and procedures while maintaining a high level of discipline throughout all stages of your development are hallmarks of an entrepreneur who is determined to stay the full distance. And remember that although your confidence and credibility levels will have been considerably enhanced since your first business plan, this next phase in your development is equally important, and the stakes are a good deal higher. So, as before, do it, but do it properly. Bring those attributes of thoroughness, professionalism, preparation and determination fully into play. In business today you have to be riding the horse out all of the time—you can never take success for granted.

Growth Options

In formulating a strategy for the future development of your business you should give consideration to a wide range of different possibilities. At the end of the day the path you choose to take will depend very much on the nature of your business and on the management and financial resources you can bring to bear on the situation. In broad terms, the following growth options should be considered.

1. Organic Growth

This entails making further investments in your core business and increasing the pace of your existing activities, through embarking on some or all of the following courses of action:

- Increasing the level of sales resources in order to achieve greater market penetration. This would only make sense where you are satisfied that there is additional untapped profitable business to be secured in your existing markets and market sectors.

- Repositioning your existing sales effort in order to focus more strongly on high-yielding products or services, fast movers, and better-performing market sectors, and on more profitable customer types and geographical areas. Remember that enhancing the performance of the business is all about improving the bottom line—not just increasing revenues.

- Identifying and opening up new markets for your products and services. This is an obvious and logical step to consider, but care should be taken to properly research and interpret all new markets and satisfy yourself that you fully understand their different characteristics and that you can adapt your products or services and your sales strategy to meet the changed situation. Entering into a trading relationship with another company or companies can be an effective and appropriate way of breaking into overseas markets. Embarking on any expansion programme entails putting your money, usually in large quantities, at risk, and distance from your home base together with different languages and business cultures will compound the commercial and financial risks involved. The use of suitable local distributors in overseas markets should be considered as a first step in order to minimise these risks.

- Expanding your range of products or services in order to generate a wider spread of sales revenues. This could be an attractive option, especially where those new offerings can be aimed at your customer base and channelled through your existing sales and distribution network. Consideration must of course be given to the level of investment needed for plant, machinery and production facilities and to acquiring the necessary people skills and expertise.

- Improving the profit margin on your products and services, either through increased prices or achieving greater cost efficiencies, or both. This review should be conducted on a regular basis, but by incorporating it into your expansion plan you will highlight its importance as one of the ways of improving the overall performance of the business. Furthermore, your decision to embark on an expansionary path makes it imperative that you maintain, and where possible improve, your level of competitiveness.

2. Joint Ventures

A joint venture arrangement is becoming an increasingly popular form of enterprise development. It entails two or more partners integrating part of their activities into some form of jointly run operation. Under the right conditions, the matching of two sets of complementary business strengths will be the correct strategy to adopt, as it should lead to greater opportunities and a stronger presence than would otherwise be the case if the parties concerned were to operate independently.

There are a variety of reasons for considering the possibility of a joint venture arrangement with another partner, including the following:

- Penetration of a new geographical market.

  In setting out to break into new overseas markets, you may wish to consider linking up with an enterprise that is already active in the markets in question. As an outsider you will stand to benefit from the assistance of an indigenous company that has the necessary local knowledge, goodwill, and experience. Such an arrangement could help to reduce the cultural, political and financial risks of embarking on a foreign operation.

- Spreading the risks of establishing new products or services.

A venture set up with a view to jointly manufacturing a new product or providing new services may offer a range of advantages, including

sharing of fixed costs;

achievement of economies of scale; and

raising of sufficient capital to fund the project.

- Gaining access to complementary technology and research techniques.

Co-operating with another partner in order to acquire knowledge you do not already possess may serve as an important means of transferring technology while at the same time allowing you the opportunity of making money from the sale of your own technology, mainly through licensing arrangements.

If you are giving serious consideration to the possibility of establishing a joint venture as part of your growth strategy, there are certain steps that you should take.

- You will need the assistance of an industrial development agency or consulting house to help find an appropriate partner. Before doing this, however, you must be clear in your own mind what it is you wish to achieve. In particular, spell out what you will bring to such an arrangement as well as what you hope to achieve in return.

- If you are forming a joint venture to gain access to new markets, try to ensure that your partner has the commitment to stay with the project even if the going starts to get rough.

- Very often the management of the joint venture may present the greatest problems. Where possible, select a partner with a compatible management style and complementary skills, thereby ensuring that the new venture has a broad range of expertise. Agree at the outset on the management team needed to run the joint venture. Management responsibility could be assigned to one of the partners or to a team recruited from the companies involved.

Finally, it is worth remembering from the outset that the objectives and priorities of the partners to a joint venture will tend to change over the years. Eventually it may be desirable for one company to buy out the other, or sell off the business, or even terminate it. However, in the right situation, with the right partner, and based on very specific strategic goals, a joint venture arrangement can be very successful.

3. Mergers

Finding other businesses with a sufficient degree of compatibility with your own to warrant serious merger considerations might not be that difficult; finding two owners who would be prepared to allow it to happen would be. Nevertheless, it should not be ruled out as a viable option, because with the right partner and combination of businesses it could make a great deal of sense. The ideal situation is where the profile of the partner company runs along the following lines:

- The operation is roughly the same size as your own and at a similar stage of development.

- The products or services being offered are complementary to your own.

- There is a need to open up new and larger markets.

- There is enough synergy between the two operations to considerably enhance the prospects for both businesses in a merged operation.

The potential benefits to be derived from merging your business with a suitable partner can be summarised as follows:

Greater economies of scale

Broader range of products or services

Combined forces making it easier to compete in new markets

Rationalisation leading to cost savings

Stronger management team

No money need change hands; instead, ownership of the merged entity can be determined on the basis of the relative net worth of the companies involved.

At the end of the day, the potential for such an arrangement will depend on whether the entrepreneurs concerned believe that the benefits accruing from a single merged entity are enough to outweigh the perceived disadvantages of relinquishing autonomy and self-determination. Looked at on purely commercial grounds, however, it is an option that should be given some serious consideration.

4. Acquisitions

Growth by acquisition is an obvious and often tempting option. It is also a high-risk strategy, as is evidenced by the number of well-known and highly publicised failures of recent times. It is in many ways the simplest option to bring to fruition, but the hardest to manage thereafter.

Before contemplating any move into the acquisition arena you should therefore carry out a rigorous self-assessment to determine whether your business is capable of making and subsequently handling such a move. Ask yourself the following pertinent questions:

Has my business a strong managerial competence?

Have we the required financial strength or access to the necessary funding without causing any undue strain?

Can we devote the substantial amount of time and effort needed to find a suitable acquisition candidate without adversely affecting our existing operations?

Have we the financial reporting systems and the organisational structures necessary to integrate the acquired company quickly?

Have we the support and surveillance staff to put in place in order to assess and develop the acquired company?

Have we the ability and the resources to absorb any setbacks?

Will I have the support of my board and of my investors?

If objectively you can answer these questions in the affirmative, then the next step will be to consider the type of acquisition you wish to make and your reasons for doing so. Broadly speaking, there are two main types of acquisition:

(1) A commercial acquisition, deriving from the needs of your existing business. These would include the need for new markets, new technology, control of outlets or sources of raw materials, and additional management

resources. In general, the acquisition of an established company in your own sector will often turn out to be the safest and most economical method of expanding into new markets. Buying market share is normally cheaper than fighting for it.

(2) A diversification acquisition, to spread risk through the development of opportunities and dependence based on new business areas. However, risk spreading through diversification can often prove to be a double-edged sword. Unless you have a lot of business management mileage under your bonnet, I would strongly advise sticking to what you know when expanding your operations. Past experience has shown that in general, the closer the field of activity of the acquisition to the core business, the greater the chance of success.

Following this self-assessment, the task of setting out the criteria and the parameters for the acquisition should be undertaken, taking into account both your objectives and your capabilities. The criteria set should cover the following subjects at least:

Type of business sought

Industry sector

Size definition

Geographical scope

State of financial health

Labour intensity

Management ability

Once you have set out your acquisition criteria, it is important that you stick to them. Otherwise there is a danger that the importance of the criteria will tend to be forgotten or lost in the excitement of the chase.

A systematic search to identify suitable acquisition candidates is a concentrated and time-consuming exercise and one that you should not undertake yourself. There are several sources of help available, including:

Major accountancy firms

Management consultants

Stockbrokers

Merchant banks

Business brokers

Some of these organisations will maintain a register of companies for sale or prepared to consider an approach. Others will undertake to research a market segment to identify suitable companies and then approach them. All work should be undertaken for an agreed fee.

When the potential targets have been reduced to, say, one serious contender, consideration in depth of that target must be undertaken. The more information obtained and considered before the contract is agreed, the greater the chances of success. The objective at this stage must be to obtain as complete a picture of the target as possible, for the purposes of:

● assessing its future prospects;

● considering the areas of risk;

● providing a plan for post-acquisition action;

● providing ammunition for the negotiators;

● establishing a price bracket.

In the completion of any acquisition, price will obviously be an important issue. However, it is worth remembering that the prime factor should be the quality of the business being acquired and the ability to extract value from it. It is worth paying a realistic price for a good business rather than a knock-down price for a bad business requiring a difficult turn-round and absorbing both management time and money.

Finally, if you have serious doubts about the acquisition, then walk away from it. A bad purchase is a good deal worse than none at all.

Summary

The following is a summary of the sequence of events that should be followed in embarking on a growth phase for the expansion and on-going development of your business:

1. Ensure that the basic business is properly off the ground and firmly established on solid foundations. Check for the obvious signs that this is in fact so.

2. Begin the process of formulating strategies for future growth and expansion of the business at board level.

3. Give consideration to a wide range of growth options, including organic growth, joint ventures, mergers, and acquisitions.

4. Refer all detailed examination of the main options to a specially appointed committee with specific and clearly defined terms of reference.

5. See that the committee's detailed reviews are referred back for further consideration at board level and for decisions to be taken.

6. Prepare and agree a detailed business plan in respect of the preferred option.

7. Don't fall into the trap of expanding just for size. Instead, focus primarily on achieving quality

and value.

8.   Implement the chosen growth strategy in the same rigorous fashion and with the same degree of determination, thoroughness and professionalism with which you went about establishing your business in the first instance.

12

Managing Growth

Making the change from a fledgling operation to a business with ambitious expansion plans and growth targets is going to involve a large culture shock, which will have an impact on all areas of your company.

As an entrepreneur, you faced a huge challenge when you set out to go into business on your own. What you will now be faced with is a challenge of a different kind but one that is at least as difficult and perhaps one that you may be even less prepared or trained for. It entails the management of the transition from being a small, personalised operation, propelled in the main by your own individual entrepreneurial spirit and passion, to donning the mantle of a more mature business, which is committed to growth and expansion and with a requirement to be structured and run on a more conventional corporate basis. The gap between the two states is a very big one indeed, but it must be bridged.

The first and most important thing is that you recognise that there is such a gap and that you must address it and that in addressing it you are going to have to make considerable changes to the way you organise and run your business. Before considering what these changes will entail, let us first examine some of the strengths and weaknesses of a typical small business in its early years of operation, to get a better understanding of why it is unrealistic to assume that such an arrangement could be expected to support a business now entering a new growth phase and having to perform in a more expansion-driven environment.

1.   The main impetus behind getting your business off the ground will have come from your own personal drive, energy, and commitment. This entrepreneurial spirit and dedication inevitably rubs off on the other members of the team, and is often characterised by a willingness on the part of the staff to put in long hours, perform in a variety of different roles, and display a commitment and a level of application that is often above and beyond the call of duty. However, this degree of unswerving loyalty and dedication to duty cannot be sustained indefinitely.

2.   The management skills needed to operate a fast-growing business will be more sophisticated and much more demanding than those required for a small-scale operation. There will be a greater need to focus on such aspects as planning, organisation, motivation and communication than was required heretofore.

3.   The level of investment in all areas of the business, from production facilities and people

resources to marketing, training, and promotional support, will need to be reviewed and upgraded in order to properly reflect the requirements of your changing operating environment.

4. When a business is in its infancy and at a high-risk stage, everybody involved is seen to be at the same level and in the same boat. As the business becomes more established and begins to be successful and profitable, people's attitudes will begin to change. You yourself, as the principal owner and beneficiary, will be looked at in a different light. I remember getting a considerable shock when one of my colleagues announced that he didn't see why he should work as hard as me when he didn't have anything like as much to gain from the resultant continuing success of the business. Such is human nature. While only a minority of people want to undertake the initial high-risk investment, once that investment starts to look inspired then everyone will be laying claims to a slice of the action. You are going to have to cope with what may seem to you an unreasonable attitude and devise ways and means of addressing it.

5. Similarly, people who in the early days were only concerned with getting the job done will now, in a more expansionary and mature environment, begin to look to matters of personal importance, such as status, level of pay, promotion prospects, job security, pension entitlement, and holiday arrangements. These are normal, natural and healthy aspirations and

must be taken into consideration. There will occasionally be situations where a spouse is the person pulling some of these strings, which may lead to additional pressures and give rise to somewhat exaggerated levels of expectation. Your task will be to assess the true worth and capacity of your people, based on your estimation of their capabilities, and not to be pressured into making appointments and awards that are not in the best interests of the company.

So let's take a look at the kind of changes you are going to have to implement if you are to position your company to meet the new challenges that will face it as it embarks on a new and exciting phase of expansion and growth.

1. The first task is to take steps to ensure that you can pull back from being heavily involved in the day-to-day operational aspects of the business. This will entail acceptance of the principle of delegation—something you will probably feel a little uneasy about at first but which is an essential prerequisite to making the transition. Your own involvement from here on must be increasingly concerned with providing strong overall management, leadership, motivation and communication to your staff while at the same time planning the development and expansion of your business and carefully monitoring its progress and performance.

2. This requirement to delegate, together with the demands placed on the business as a result of its expansion, will necessitate putting a strong management team in place. In doing this, be

careful to select people who are not just good at their jobs but who either are, or have demonstrated a potential to be, good managers, and who will be able to organise, control and motivate others to achieve results. Where you feel it necessary, invest in management training programmes to raise the standards of performance. Spending time and money in this area is a wise investment, as a strong, effective management is a prerequisite to securing and supporting an expanding business. Managers must be seen as the wealth and profit creators in any business.

3. Review your resource requirements in all areas of the business, both in terms of people, machinery, equipment, and skills. In doing so, examine different ways and means of streamlining production and improving efficiency. Don't just throw money at the business: at every stage of your development be determined to get the best possible return for your additional investment. Growing for the sake of growing is not on. You must ensure that your productivity levels are being steadily improved and that increased turnover is bringing with it improved levels of profitability.

4. Put the necessary funding package in place to finance your growth targets. Having prepared a business expansion proposal, meet with your financial advisers and seek their advice and assistance in obtaining the most cost-effective way of financing the development of your business. You will now have at least one important perceived advantage from a financier's

viewpoint that you didn't have when you started out, and that is, a greater degree of credibility, resulting from a tried and proven track record in running your own business. So use your improved bargaining position and shop around to get the best possible financing deal.

5. Carry out a review of your management control and financial reporting systems and ensure that these are upgraded in line with the changing nature and pace of the business. This will almost certainly entail additional investment in computer technology and the implementation of more advanced management information systems.

6. Review the remuneration package and terms of employment for all your top employees. In order to entice and retain the best people, you are going to have to pay top rates. Where possible, incorporate a strong element of performance-related payments, such as bonuses and profit-sharing, as part of the rewards package. For your key people, give consideration to the introduction of a share option scheme, with the possibility of extending this to other members of the staff as your business evolves. This will involve the issuing of new shares, thereby diluting, in the short term, the value of existing shareholdings. However, if the people concerned are good enough and critical to the continuing success and profitability of the business, then all investors will stand to gain in the long run. Make sure you get contracts of employment signed and in place for all your key people, and most particularly in respect of those who have

been given a slice of the action. Such contracts should typically be for three to five-year periods.

7.   Set about beefing up your board of directors. If it consists only of the original founder-directors, consideration should be given to appointing at least one and possibly more outside people who will be qualified to make a significant contribution to strategic planning and to the management and control of the company's future direction and development. Don't just seek out important names: you will need experienced businesspeople who are willing to take an active interest and involvement in the company's affairs and whose expertise, track record and contacts could prove invaluable in helping to charter and secure the future success of the business.

13

Securing the Future

If you have been running a successful business, one that has achieved several years of profitable and sustainable growth, then you will be enjoying both a high level of personal satisfaction and a warm feeling of financial well-being. You will also be acutely aware that you are now sitting on a valuable and increasingly more marketable asset. There are two important implications that stem from this, one of which has strong benefits for the continuing funding requirements of the company, and the other which has a positive bearing on your own financial security and that of your fellow-shareholders. Let us consider each of these in turn.

1. Running a business with a strong profits record and good growth prospects will not only result in enhanced shareholder valuations but, more significantly, it increases the attractiveness of the company to potential outside investors. Should you wish to exercise it, you now have an additional funding option, namely, the placing of new shares, either privately or publicly, for the purpose of financing further expansion of

the business or reducing your level of debt, or both.

While accepting that by doing so you may be temporarily diluting the value of existing shareholdings in the company, it does offer an important advantage, in that it gives you access to investment capital without any corresponding interest payments burden. If the funds raised are put to productive use, then the effect will be either to add strength to the balance sheet in the short term or to further enhance the inherent value of the business over the medium to long term.

2.   A business that you started from scratch some years previously will by now have transformed your own financial circumstances and made you a relatively wealthy person, at least on paper. As the major investor, you may at some stage wish to consider reducing your shareholding in the business in order to make provision for your own future financial security and that of your family.

Such a step should not be interpreted as representing either a falling off of confidence in or commitment to the business. On the contrary, having resolutely adopted a prudent approach to the management of your business affairs, you also have a duty to similarly safeguard your own personal financial security. I would recommend any entrepreneur who has reached a certain level of business success, and under the right circumstances and conditions, to give serious consideration to cashing in at least some of the chips, both to provide for the future and to see something tangible for your efforts and achievements.

Should you wish to pursue either of the above objectives then there are two main options open to you, as follows :

1. Private Placing

This entails arranging for some of the existing or of newly issued shares in the business to be placed, through a firm of stockbrokers, with selected private investors or with one of a range of investment or financial institutions, such as investment banks, insurance corporations, or development capital companies.

In the case of some of these investors they will be satisfied to operate as sleeping partners, seeking a good return on their investment but content to leave the running of the business to you and your fellow-directors. On the other hand, if you wish to involve, say, the corporate investment arm of one of the major banks, they will usually prefer to play a more active role in the development of the business, and will wish to have board representation. This can be an added advantage, in that it contributes both financial muscle and business expertise to your operation, while at the same time making you more accountable and helping to keep everybody concerned with the business on their toes.

2. Public Flotation

This involves taking your company into the public domain through a flotation of your shares on the stock market. From the point of view of maximising the value of the company this is certainly the best route to take, as, with the right business credentials and in a positive investment climate, the multiple of earnings paid for public companies will usually be higher than that under a private placement. However, it is not an option that I would recommend lightly unless you have a well-developed and mature business with a broad spread of activities and a very soundly based and expansive future.

Over the past decade a large number of small companies have been brought to the market with high expectations and ambitious plans and surrounded by lots of hype and media attention. While there have been some notable successes, the majority of these businesses have either underperformed or failed altogether. As a result, many private and institutional investors have had their fingers badly burnt, which has led to a greatly diminished appetite among the investment community for small-company flotations. Many such publicly quoted small companies are now considered highly speculative, making their shares more difficult to trade and leading to a situation where the vast bulk of investment funds finds its way into the larger and more liquid stocks.

As a result, one of the original and most important advantages of taking your company to the stock market—the ability to use your shares to fund acquisitions and facilitate expansion—is no longer as attractive an option for many small companies. Furthermore, the pressure of running your business and delivering results in the full glare of the public arena can be unsettling, while endeavouring to meet the demanding and ever-increasing profit growth expectations of the stock market can put enormous strains and pressures on management, often tempting them into making decisions that court short-term popularity at the expense of longer-term considerations and interests.

On balance, therefore, if you do wish to attract funds for the purpose of financing expansion or redeeming part of your investment, or both, I would recommend the private rather then the public issue route. While your company shares might not command as high a rating, the benefits of being able to run your business in private and being answerable to a smaller number of visible investors will, for most entrepreneurs, be worth it.

You have, of course, a further option: that of selling out altogether. This may seem at first glance to be a drastic step to take, but in the United States it is quite common for entrepreneurs to sell their businesses once they have brought them to a certain stage of development. I believe we are going to see this option exercised more in this part of the world as entrepreneurs seek to avoid the risks of being immersed totally in their business operations or wish to exercise the freedom, flexibility and independence to explore new opportunities and interests and take on fresh challenges.

The decision on whether to sell and move into something else will be a personal one, with no hard and fast rules applying. However, if you are growing restless in your present environment and are no longer getting the same buzz and excitement as before, and provided you have confidence in your abilities as a businessperson and can turn your hand to other ventures, then it is an option worth contemplating.

In any event, whether you choose to liquidate your investment in part or in whole, you certainly have no cause to offer any apologies for succeeding in business and for having made a lot of money in the process. As an entrepreneur, you have taken great risks, generated new wealth, created additional employment, given good service to your customers, looked after your employees, paid your suppliers, set high standards of performance, and worked long and hard. Enterprise needs to be acknowledged, encouraged, supported, promoted, and rewarded, not knocked. I am constantly amazed at how in this part of the world we are quick to jump to our feet to applaud good performances in the world of sport, entertainment, or the arts. We are proud of, and readily acknowledge, the successes of our footballers, boxers, athletes, writers, poets, actors, and singers. This of course is as it should be. But when it comes to business in general, and to successful enterprise in particular, the public perception is generally one of suspicion, and the climate is antagonistic. Yet a successful business run on a professional basis and performing to high standards is of far greater importance and significance to the life blood of our economic well-being, although this is seldom acknowledged and rarely appreciated.

This public antipathy to successful businesspeople must change. We need many, many more entrepreneurs and a healthier entrepreneurial climate if living standards are to be raised and the employment expectations of society are to be met.

In my book, each and every entrepreneur deserves to be applauded and rewarded for his or her courage in getting up off their bottom and creating a new enterprise, for the risks they take in doing so, for the initiative they display, for their energy, commitment, and drive, and for their contribution to wealth creation and to the employment needs of our society. So, enjoy your success and the fruits of your endeavours, and damn the begrudgers!